In HIS Light

A 31-Day Devotional
Guidance, Protection, and Love

stephanie d. moore

Edited by
Debra M. Smith

But **everything** exposed by the light becomes **visible**
—and everything that is **illuminated**
becomes a light.
Ephesians 5:13

Copyright © 2023 by Stephanie D. Moore

Published by
Moore Marketing and Communications, LLC

Kansas City, Missouri
StephanieDMoore.com
MooretoRead.com

In accordance with the U.S. Copyright Act of 1976, scanning, uploading, or electronic sharing of any part of this book, audio, written, or e-published is strictly prohibited and unlawful. No part of this book may be reproduced in any form by any means, including photocopying, electronic, mechanical, recording, or by any information storage and retrieval systems without permission in writing by the copyright owner.

Bulk copies or group sales of this book are available by contacting Stephanie D. Moore at moore@stephaniedmoore.com or (405) 306-9833.

Moore, Stephanie D.
In His Light: A 31-Day Devotional on His Guidance, Protection, and Love

Edited by Debra M. Smith

First Edition Printed September 2023
Printed in the USA.

Cover Design and Layout Design by
Moore Marketing and Communications, LLC.
All Rights Reserved.

Cover Photo used in design retrieved at pexels.com, taken by Kindel Media.

ISBN: 978-1-955544-32-0

In him was life, and that life was the light of all mankind. The light shines in the darkness, and the darkness has not overcome it.

John 1:4-5

In HIS Light

A 31-Day Devotional
Guidance, Protection, and Love

stephanie d moore
Edited by
Debra M. Smith

Day 1	Reflection	9
Day 2	Wisdom	13
Day 3	Humility and Humiliation	15
Day 4	His Presence is Light	19
Day 5	The Lord is My Light	21
Day 6	Risk Everything	25
Day 7	Let God Do It	29
Day 8	A Day Known Only to the Lord	33
Day 9	The Lord Turns Our Darkness Into Light	37
Day 10	Never Alone	41
Day 11	Rule in the Fear of God	45
Day 12	The Protection of God	49
Day 13	God Will Never Disappoint	53
Day 14	Armor of Light	55
Day 15	Share Your Light With Others	57
Day 16	Called Out of Darkness	59
Day 17	Tried By Fire	61
Day 18	Joy, Wisdom & Enlightenment	65
Day 19	Acutely Awarea	69
Day 20	Jesus at the Head	73
Day 21	In Your Light	77
Day 22	A New Walk	79
Day 23	Light is Love	83
Day 24	Speak Light	87
Day 25	The Light of God	91
Day 26	Freedom	95
Day 27	The God of More than Enough	99
Day 28	From Darkness to Light	101
Day 29	Our God is a Consuming Fire	105
Day 30	A Witness to the Light	109
Day 31	The Nature of Darkness	113
Citations		115

In Loving Memory

Allan "Grip" Smith

We always triumph through Christ
when people witness the effect
of the knowledge of Christ in our lives
everywhere we go.

2 Corinthians 2:14

Reflection

> But everything exposed by the light becomes visible—and everything that is illuminated becomes a light.
>
> Ephesians 5:13

I grew up in the church. From the time I was a little girl, I sang "Jesus loves me this I know for the Bible tells me so!" But as I matured, I was immersed in unspeakable acts of abuse, abandonment, and abject poverty. I recognized that we did not all live the same reality. My family was different and more importantly, I was different. But all I ever wanted was to desperately fit in. I wanted to be loved like we sang about in church. I wanted it to feel like it sounded, innocent and sweet.

Jesus came that we all may have the opportunity to experience unconditional love. What we sang about was true but it took me 30 years to realize it. I could only identify God's love when my love of self disappeared. I'd finally recognized that all my ideas weren't right, healthy, or true. At the same time, everything God promised came to pass. Not what I desired, but everything he promised. No weapon formed prospered. Even when the worst weapon of all was my destructive thinking.

We all desire to be seen, heard, and understood. Jesus

In HIS Light

meets us where we are and he lets us know in very intimate ways that he can see, hear, and understand what we are experiencing. Once we are able to see God, he begins to guide us that we might share his love with others.

When we stand in the light of God, we reflect his light. Our only desire becomes to please him because he has proven himself to be faithful and loving. We learn to reciprocate what we are given when we know the giver's motivation is sincere and heartfelt.

Likewise, God desires to be seen in us - in our actions, words, and thoughts.

> For you were once darkness, but now you are light in the Lord. Live as children of light (for the fruit of the light consists in all goodness, righteousness and truth) and find out what pleases the Lord. Have nothing to do with the fruitless deeds of darkness, but rather expose them. It is shameful even to mention what the disobedient do in secret.
> Ephesians 5:8-12

Our light grows as we expose ourselves to God and allow his presence to saturate our being, in his light we become more like him each day. Loving Christ means that we love others and ourselves enough to forgive others and ourselves when we fall. We take it day by day, line by line, and precept by precept. We live one breath at a time and pray that we get it right today.

In HIS Light

We choose to walk with Jesus that we may grow in His Light.

Most Gracious and Heavenly Father,

We praise you and thank you for your endless love, mercy, and grace.
For with you is the fountain of life; in your light we see light. [1]
For God, who said, "Let light shine out of darkness,"
made his light shine in our hearts to give us the light
of the knowledge of God's glory displayed in the face of Christ. [2]
For light shines on the righteous and joy on the upright in heart. [3]
In the same way, let our light shine before others,
that they may see our good deeds and glorify our Father in heaven. [4]

In Jesus Name,
Amen

Wisdom

I saw that wisdom is better than folly, just as light is better than darkness.
Ecclesiastes 2:13

God plants us in darkness. A seed germinates beneath the dirt, desperate for water and light. It only grows when it is in the right environment, watered well, and receives adequate light. We much like the seed can only grow through exposure to God (light), Jesus (the Word) and the Holy Spirit (water). His Word (written and spoken) must become our environment.

As our exposure to the Godhead increases, we learn to turn our battles over to the Lord. We learn to give our burdens to the Lord. We learn to walk by faith and not by sight. With wisdom, comes rest.

I have learned to become less that God may become more in my life. We have to make room for increase, if our lives are constantly filled with what we do today, we can never grow to a level of increase for tomorrow.

It is time for many of us to let go and let God. The fool and the wise have the same fate - they both die. No matter what one has decided to embrace in life, both come to the same end. So, why not let go of the endless turmoil to become wise in our own

In HIS Light

eyes and allow God to become more and live through us that his will may be done in the earth? This is true wisdom.

We choose to walk with Jesus that we may grow in His Light.

Most Gracious and Heavenly Father,

We praise you and thank you for your endless love, mercy, and grace.
For with you is the fountain of life; in your light we see light. [1]
For God, who said, "Let light shine out of darkness,"
made his light shine in our hearts to give us the light
of the knowledge of God's glory displayed in the face of Christ. [2]
For light shines on the righteous and joy on the upright in heart. [3]
In the same way, let our light shine before others,
that they may see our good deeds and glorify our Father in heaven. [4]

In Jesus Name,
Amen

Humility and Humiliation

And God said, "Let there be light," and there was light. God saw that the light was good, and he separated the light from the darkness.

Genesis 1:3-4

I work for a notable personal injury law firm. Our primary goal is to ensure our clients (potential, new, and old) are valued, understood, and heard so we may respond and represent them appropriately.

The first step in forming a relationship with the client is to develop trust. This begins by shining a light on injustice and saying, this action and activity is unjust. We are experienced enough to navigate these waters and we want to help you. But a person must believe what we promise.

Trust is necessary to ensure that the purpose of shining a light in darkness is met with an appropriate response - separation or discontinuation of specific actions or activities.

What has been hidden, confusing, misunderstood, and questionable becomes clear in the light. But the journey to exposure, through exposure, and completing exposure is complex and often teeters between humility and humiliation.

In HIS Light

Jesus dared to live a life that reflected God's values among religious leaders and the communities they served. His image tumbled back and forth between the life-giving savior and the blasphemous whoremonger galavanting among sinners. In it all, he was doing the will of God, but those who witnessed his actions misunderstood him. They could only process his actions from their vantage point.

Jesus was considered humble by those who enjoyed his teachings, experienced his miracles, and received his healing. But Jesus was often subjected to humiliation by those who hated his teachings, doubted his sonship, and were jealous of his supernatural abilities.

Flocks of people would journey to hear Jesus preach and would bask for hours under his voice. They could see his heart through his actions and his words. This troubled those who desired to have the same impact. So the religious leaders plotted to kill him. They bribed one of his closest companions, a disciple, and captured him.

They beat Jesus, berated him, dragged him through town bloodied and worn, then hung him on a cross to die the death of those who'd committed the worst crimes. All because he shined a light in the darkness.

The journey to justice can be lonely, humiliating, and unfair. But like those who dare to trust our law firm to represent them, we can trust Jesus, who uniquely understands our journey and is committed to representing us to the end.

In HIS Light

We choose to walk with Jesus that we may grow in His Light.

Most Gracious and Heavenly Father,

We praise you and thank you for your endless love, mercy, and grace.
For with you is the fountain of life; in your light we see light. [1]
For God, who said, "Let light shine out of darkness,"
made his light shine in our hearts to give us the light
of the knowledge of God's glory displayed in the face of Christ. [2]
For light shines on the righteous and joy on the upright in heart. [3]
In the same way, let our light shine before others,
that they may see our good deeds and glorify our Father in heaven. [4]

In Jesus Name,
Amen

His Presence is Light

How I long for the months gone by, for the days when God watched over me,
when his lamp shone on my head and by his light I walked through darkness!
Job 29:2-3

With God, all things are possible. Jesus left us the gift of the Holy Spirit to empower us to be and become all that God has ordained. Job was a servant of God who recognized this.

Job walked with God, day and night. Job prayed for his family each morning, he was an amazing steward of God's blessings, and he watched over those who served him with kindness and care. In all of this, God blessed Job immensely. He had a hedge of protection around Job.

But Job also experienced immense hardship and was tested beyond measure. At one point, he lost it all and was mocked by his friends and family, who accused Job of committing a great offense against God to deserve such hardship. But Job never lost his faith in God. He never waivered in his respect or belief that God was good. Even when he lost everything he loved, he held on to his most precious gift - his relationship with God.

At one point, during the hardship, Job wished he were

In HIS Light

never born. His anguish was intense and he just could not reconcile how things had gone from so good to so bad in such a quick amount of time. Not only was Job heartbroken, he was confused. He missed the light of God that guided him each day, and helped him to navigate through life's toughest terrains. Job missed the presence of God.

When I am down, lonely, and sinking into depression, I listen to the Word of God or I turn on gospel music to help lift me. There is a light that exists in the presence of God that helps us to face every downfall. It helps us to keep going regardless of the negative circumstances that surround us. The light of the Lord reminds us that we are not alone and that every battle we are faced with belongs to the Lord.

We choose to walk with Jesus that we may grow in His Light.

Most Gracious and Heavenly Father,

We praise you and thank you for your endless love, mercy, and grace. For with you is the fountain of life; in your light we see light. [1]
For God, who said, "Let light shine out of darkness," made his light shine in our hearts to give us the light of the knowledge of God's glory displayed in the face of Christ. [2]
For light shines on the righteous and joy on the upright in heart. [3]
In the same way, let our light shine before others, that they may see our good deeds and glorify our Father in heaven. [4]

In Jesus Name,
Amen

The Lord is My Light

Do not gloat over me, my enemy! Though I have fallen, I will rise. Though I sit in darkness, the Lord will be my light.

Micah 7:8

When babies transition into toddlers, they often fall as they learn to walk. Much like babies, as we mature, we often fall, learning to walk with God. It's not the same as before, when we didn't know God or recognize our experience of God's love, mercy, and grace.

As Christians, we see God at work in our lives and we do our best to respond with appropriate reverence and a form of reciprocity. We try to be all that God desires for us to be.

But as we learn to walk, we fall. Truth be told, even if we have been walking for a while, we still fall when met with difficult circumstance.

Consider Moses. Moses spent an enormous amount of time with God and was tasked with leading the Israelites out of Egypt and into their promised land. But during the journey, God gave Moses specific instructions to give the people water while traveling. But because the people were unsatisfied and

In HIS Light

grumbling, Moses did what he knew in the past to work as opposed to what God told him to do. His anger in that one moment prevented him from entering into the promised land.

We are to be a reflection of God everywhere that we go and in all that we do. This is not an easy task as environments we are often immersed in do not welcome the Spirit of God. When we walk in the door, filled with the Spirit, intending to be lights in the world we can be met with the darkest of forces. If we are not careful, armed properly, or discerning, we can fall privy and return evil for evil which is not of God or God's desire.

We are not babies learning to walk. We have been taught how to walk and God expects us to do what he says, not what makes us comfortable. God has shined a light on us, it is up to us to reflect him everywhere that we go and in all that we do.

It does not mean that we have to be perfect. It does mean that we must do our best to walk in obedience to him. We are walking in a world that is filled with darkness and we are tasked with carrying the light of God into those places.

Moses understood his failures and course-corrected. God offers us second-chances, opportunities to get back up and try again. Though our enemies may see us stumbling along, we will cross the finish line with victory because God is for us, therefore who could be against us? His mercy endures forever.

In HIS Light

We choose to walk with Jesus that we may grow in His Light.

Most Gracious and Heavenly Father,

*We praise you and thank you for your endless love, mercy, and grace.
For with you is the fountain of life; in your light we see light.* [1]
*For God, who said, "Let light shine out of darkness,"
made his light shine in our hearts to give us the light
of the knowledge of God's glory displayed in the face of Christ.* [2]
For light shines on the righteous and joy on the upright in heart. [3]
*In the same way, let our light shine before others,
that they may see our good deeds and glorify our Father in heaven.* [4]

*In Jesus Name,
Amen*

Risk Everything

> When Jesus spoke again to the people, he said, "I am the light of the world. Whoever follows me will never walk in darkness, but will have the light of life."
>
> John 8:12

Standing with God is not always easy. But in theory, we often believe it should be. God is love, right? Even still, walking with God can be all the more difficult. Yes, without a doubt, we exercise faith in all that we do and everywhere that we go. But our faith and obedience to God can require we share the unpopular messages, do the uncommon things, and shine a light in dark and dangerous places.

As we stand, we convince ourselves that the Lord is on our side and we choose to live a life that honors him. But when we walk, we take what we believe in places where that belief may not be supported or appreciated. We run the risk of objection, rejection, and persecution.

Jesus himself faced the same challenges we face today. He often spoke in the temple teaching what he received from God the Father. He healed people on the Sabbath day. He spent time with the people the religious leaders considered unworthy, unholy, and unsaved.

In HIS Light

"Why is my language not clear to you?
Because you are unable to hear what I say."
John 8:43

Jesus experienced disrespect, hatred, and violence. He was not accepted as the Savior by most of the members of his family, he was betrayed by one of his closest confidants, and was crucified by those who professed to be good people.

Yet Jesus promises that if we follow him we will never walk in darkness. In the Greek translation it reads "never, no, never." This begs the question, what is darkness?

Darkness is defined as the absence of light. It is also defined as wickedness.

We are to stay in the will of God, doing what pleases him. Therefore, we sever our participation, contribution, and connection to darkness.

This can only be accomplished if we are brave enough to follow Jesus. When we follow Jesus we are filled with his unconditional love, mercy, and grace. He goes before us and makes every crooked place straight. We not only share his message, we share his presence which gives life to those who need him.

Walking with Jesus requires we trust him enough to risk everything.

In HIS Light

We choose to walk with Jesus that we may grow in His Light.

Most Gracious and Heavenly Father,

We praise you and thank you for your endless love, mercy, and grace.
For with you is the fountain of life; in your light we see light. [1]
For God, who said, "Let light shine out of darkness,"
made his light shine in our hearts to give us the light
of the knowledge of God's glory displayed in the face of Christ. [2]
For light shines on the righteous and joy on the upright in heart. [3]
In the same way, let our light shine before others,
that they may see our good deeds and glorify our Father in heaven. [4]

In Jesus Name,
Amen

Let God Do It

By day the Lord went ahead of them in a pillar of cloud to guide them on their way and by night in a pillar of fire to give them light, so that they could travel by day or night. Neither the pillar of cloud by day nor the pillar of fire by night left its place in front of the people.

———————

Then the angel of God, who had been traveling in front of Israel's army, withdrew and went behind them. The pillar of cloud also moved from in front and stood behind them, coming between the armies of Egypt and Israel. Throughout the night the cloud brought darkness to the one side and light to the other side; so neither went near the other all night long.

Exodus 13:20-21, 14:19-20

The battle belongs to God. When we walk with God, taking light into places of darkness, exposing the work of the enemy, we will suffer attack. But God is our help. He guides us and protects us.

The Israelites were subjected to hard slavery for many years, oppressed and without a way of escape. They cried to God for relief from their burdens. Moses came and demanded for Pharoah to let the Israelites go free to worship their God. Pharoah refused. God responded by sending several plagues, with the ultimate sentence being a death sentence to every first

In HIS Light

born male in Egypt. Then Pharaoah let the Israelites go.

God went with the people of Israel. He led them on a journey to freedom. He took them the long way, because they were not adequately prepared to go the shorter route. They were not ready for the type of battles they would have to fight for their promised land. As God led the people through Moses out of Egypt, Pharoah changed his mind and decided to pursue them. God then went from guiding them with cloud and light ahead to protecting them from behind. God also gave the Israelites a strategy to confuse their enemy. Pharoah gathered all of his troops and pursued them.

God lured the enemy out that he may receive the glory he deserved in Egypt. He destroyed Pharoah and his army to show that he was the one true living God and that no other existed beyond him.

God is the King of Kings and the Lord of Lords. There is no other god. When we face enemies that pursue us, threaten us and seek to destroy us, we can call on God, our Father in heaven and he will send his angels to encamp around us. We can look to the hills, where our help comes from, the father of lights and he will be with us wherever we go.

There is no need for us to worry, no reason to be afraid. We just need to let God do it.

In HIS Light

We choose to walk with Jesus that we may grow in His Light.

Most Gracious and Heavenly Father,

We praise you and thank you for your endless love, mercy, and grace.
For with you is the fountain of life; in your light we see light. [1]
For God, who said, "Let light shine out of darkness,"
made his light shine in our hearts to give us the light
of the knowledge of God's glory displayed in the face of Christ. [2]
For light shines on the righteous and joy on the upright in heart. [3]
In the same way, let our light shine before others,
that they may see our good deeds and glorify our Father in heaven. [4]

In Jesus Name,
Amen

A Day Known Only to the Lord

> It will be a unique day—a day known only to the Lord—with no distinction between day and night. When evening comes, there will be light.
>
> Zechariah 14:6

The Lord, who has created heaven and earth, will one day reign in Jerusalem. At that time, it will be a new earth and life as we know it, will be forever changed.

Have you ever been to a funeral? Ever looked into the casket of a loved one who was no longer living? I can remember the day I saw my grandfather lying in the casket. His body was there, but he was gone. That part of him that I loved so greatly, his laugh, his smile, his comforting words, and precious warnings... were no longer present. All that was left, was a shell of who he was.

The part of my grandfather that was missing is the very part of God that he places within us. It is his Spirit that gives us life. It is the God within us that people fall in love with, that people admire, that we form relationships with. It is the undeniable breath of life granted to us by the creator of all things.

In HIS Light

This same God, who gave us life, has the power to destroy all things that are within the earth. God loves us and desires that we live a life that brings him glory.

When we create, author, invent, or develop, we too want to get credit for the work we have done... we are like our father in heaven. But God doesn't demand credit for his work, he doesn't requite justice in ways that cause us to suffer. Instead, he gives us the ability to choose our own way and our decisions dictate our outcomes. If we choose to bless and pray for those who despitefully use us, it is our choice. If we choose to forgive those who deny their part in our demise or downfall, that is our choice. If we willingly cause ourselves harm through destructive activities such as sex out of wedlock, obsessive drinking, gambling, smoking, drug addiction and more... it is our choice.

Jesus, who sacrificed his life, died that we may not die in our sins. Yet, one thing is clear, repentance is a behavior, not a word or set of phrases one mutters to go his own way. Repentance requires a sincere relationship with God and acknowledges the death within sin and utilizes the way of escape God grants from sin when it beckons.

God, who blew the breath of life within each of us, has given us all a choice. We get to choose whom we will serve, whether it be the lust of life, man, or God himself. No matter our decision, there are specific outcomes tied to each choice. God is not a man, he will not be mocked. There will be a day when God comes to deliver his verdict and separate the light from the dark. It is up to us to decide which side we want to be on when he arrives.

In HIS Light

We choose to walk with Jesus that we may grow in His Light.

Most Gracious and Heavenly Father,

*We praise you and thank you for your endless love, mercy, and grace.
For with you is the fountain of life; in your light we see light.* [1]
*For God, who said, "Let light shine out of darkness,"
made his light shine in our hearts to give us the light
of the knowledge of God's glory displayed in the face of Christ.* [2]
For light shines on the righteous and joy on the upright in heart. [3]
*In the same way, let our light shine before others,
that they may see our good deeds and glorify our Father in heaven.* [4]

*In Jesus Name,
Amen*

The Lord Turns Our Darkness Into Light

You, Lord, are my lamp; the Lord turns my darkness into light.
2 Samuel 22:29

Moses was tasked with leading the Israelites out of Egypt and into their promised land. He walked with God day and night. Aaron served as the high priest of the Israelites. He and Moses were brothers. They trusted each other. The Lord instructed Aaron through Moses to position seven lamps, lit with the crushed oil of olives, in front of the lampstand in the tent of meeting. The tent of meeting was a consecrated area of worship to God.

The Levites were a tribe among the Israelites that were also set aside for God's service. They were to become ceremonially clean and presented to God as a wave offering. A wave offering was waved before God at the altar, rather than burning it. This waving was an indication that the entity being waved belonged to God.[5] The Levites became a consecrated portion of God's people that were dedicated in worship to God. They served as a constant light among the people.

In HIS Light

God will always separate the light from the dark. He keeps his portion set aside, well-lit, distinguished, and protected for his service. In 2 Samuel 22, David sings about such protection. David was well-known for being a mighty warrior and for his ability to worship God in song. When he was anointed to serve as the next king of Israel, Saul put a bounty on his head and was determined to kill him. But David had already been preserved for God's service, set aside, distinguished and protected.

For such protection, David began his praise to God.

"The Lord is my rock, my fortress and my deliverer; my God is my rock, in whom I take refuge, my shield and the horn of my salvation. He is my stronghold, my refuge and my savior—from violent people you save me."

2 Samuel 22:3

David found himself in a dark place, he ran from Saul and his army for years, trying his best to avoid death at his enemy's hand. David saw many die in an effort to protect him. While his anointing kept him from being killed, it did not keep him out of harm's way. David needed to call on God, depend on God, and trust God to complete the will of God.

"I called to the Lord, who is worthy of praise, and have been saved from my enemies. The waves of death swirled about me; the torrents of destruction overwhelmed me. The cords of the grave coiled around me; the snares of death confronted me."

2 Samuel 22:4-6

Like David, we must learn that as we walk through the valleys of darkness, we must lean on God every step of the way. We must activate the protection of God through strategic prayer and we must pray without ceasing. Only then can the seven lamps shine before the lampstand of our lives, separating the light from the dark. We are a wave offering, submitted before

In HIS Light

God, constantly being cleansed for service, turning our darkness into light.

> "But you are a chosen people, a royal priesthood, a holy nation, God's special possession, that you may declare the praises of him who called you out of darkness into his wonderful light."
>
> I Peter 2:9

> "The people living in darkness have seen a great light; on those living in the land of the shadow of death a light has dawned."
>
> Matthew 4:16

As the prophet Isaiah prophesied, Jesus, the true light of the world, began to preach the gospel soon after John the Baptist was imprisoned, but not before Jesus was tested in the wilderness by the devil.

We each have our own tests (much like Joseph, David, Daniel, and our Lord Jesus). But once we have been crushed, like the olives that provide the oil for the lamps that light the seven lampstands, our clean oil will light the way for many who live in darkness. Through our witness, the actions we take more so than the words we speak, many will be exposed to the power and light of the Lord, who has turned our darkness into light.

In HIS Light

We choose to walk with Jesus that we may grow in His Light.

Most Gracious and Heavenly Father,

We praise you and thank you for your endless love, mercy, and grace.
For with you is the fountain of life; in your light we see light. [1]
For God, who said, "Let light shine out of darkness,"
made his light shine in our hearts to give us the light
of the knowledge of God's glory displayed in the face of Christ. [2]
For light shines on the righteous and joy on the upright in heart. [3]
In the same way, let our light shine before others,
that they may see our good deeds and glorify our Father in heaven. [4]

In Jesus Name,
Amen

Never Alone

Even though I walk through the darkest valley, I will fear no evil, for you are with me; your rod and your staff, they comfort me.

Psalm 23:4

Companionship is a part of God's plan. He created us to commune with one another. We were never intended to live in isolation.

The LORD God said, "It is not good for the man to be alone. I will make a helper suitable for him."

Genesis 2:18

Yet, in the Bible, we see many kings, prophets and warriors who spent long periods in isolation.

Jeremiah, Moses, David, Jonah, Joseph, Samson, Elijah, and even Jesus were all alone with God for a season or seasons. When we are alone with God, we seek him while he may be found, we commune with him day and night, we learn to discern his voice that we may be prepared when surrounded by a sea of others (including our own voice which seeks comfort over godly decision-making).

In HIS Light

Sin is pervasive and It seeks to destroy each of us. Satan is the accuser of the brethren and he is subtly finding ways to accuse each of us. But God promises that he will complete the work that he began in us, so we have nothing to fear but God himself. When we sin, we must repent and turn from the wicked choices we have made that bring dishonor to God. Secret sins are no different from public sins because God sees all.

When we are alone with God, he teaches us the consequence of sin. He reveals to us his glory and invites us to commune with his Holy Spirit that the Lord may become our closest and most trusted confidant. This prepares us to walk in a world that is full of distractions, darkness, and disillusion.

> But the Helper, the Holy Spirit whom the Father will send in My name, He will teach you all things, and remind you of all that I said to you.
> John 14:26

We have nothing to fear when we walk with God. We are never alone. We are not isolated, we are in communion with the Most High God, we are one with the Holy Spirit, we are learning to live in a world that is bound for destruction and to shine a light in the darkness.

> Surely the Lord's goodness and mercy will follow us all the days of our life and we will dwell in the house of the Lord, forever.
> Psalm 23:6

In HIS Light

We choose to walk with Jesus that we may grow in His Light.

Most Gracious and Heavenly Father,

We praise you and thank you for your endless love, mercy, and grace.
For with you is the fountain of life; in your light we see light. [1]
For God, who said, "Let light shine out of darkness,"
made his light shine in our hearts to give us the light
of the knowledge of God's glory displayed in the face of Christ. [2]
For light shines on the righteous and joy on the upright in heart. [3]
In the same way, let our light shine before others,
that they may see our good deeds and glorify our Father in heaven. [4]

In Jesus Name,
Amen

Rule in the Fear of God

"The Spirit of the Lord spoke through me; his word was on my tongue. The God of Israel spoke, the Rock of Israel said to me: 'When one rules over people in righteousness, when he rules in the fear of God, he is like the light of morning at sunrise on a cloudless morning, like the brightness after rain that brings grass from the earth.'

2 Samuel 23:2-4

They say that people don't quit jobs, they quit managers.

A manager can make life in the office great, or they can make it miserable for you. No matter how hard you work, or what you do, if a manager doesn't like you, it is difficult to be motivated to work.

David, the anointed king of Israel, was son to a father who did not like him, servant to a king that wanted to kill him, and father to a son that tried to overthrow his kingdom. David was no stranger to adversity and often, those closest to him were the artisans strategically attempting to destroy his life.

The light of morning at sunrise on a cloudless morning depicts hope, peace, and joy. This is what ruling in righteousness and the fear of God looks like. People who serve others desire

In HIS Light

to walk in confidence, with a secure knowledge that those they serve respect them and therefore they want to do their best work, they desire to serve with excellence. This is the light that shines after rain which inspires growth, good managers want their staff to grow in responsibility.

David had thirty-seven faithful men, mighty warriors, strong in battle. As David named them, he highlighted three very important men. In fact, they were called "The Three." They were not important because they told David what he wanted to hear, they were important because they worked tirelessly and did not give up when David and his army were in the worst of battles. Each man had a valiant story that shared that each of them were heroes in their own right, famous among men.

But the most respected warrior, who was chief over "The Three" was just as famous and for more valiant works, his name was Abishai the brother of Joab son of Zeruiah.

Benaiah, who was not the chief nor among the three highest warriors was honorably mentioned. He was known for killing a lion in a pit on a snowy day, and attacking a large spear-tauting Egyptian with only a club and determination as his guide, Benaiah was also equally as famous as the three and named David's bodyguard.

There were 37 honorable men that would go with David into battle anywhere and anytime.

People who love and respect leadership go out of their way to do an excellent job for good leaders. But leaders who fail are often avoided like the plague, unable to get the work that is necessary done, they do not give hope but operate as leaders from a place of fear.

In HIS Light

As God calls us to serve Him, we must elect to do so with excellence. We must operate in leadership from a place of humility, wisdom, and confidence that only God can give.

We choose to walk with Jesus that we may grow in His Light.

Most Gracious and Heavenly Father,

We praise you and thank you for your endless love, mercy, and grace.
For with you is the fountain of life; in your light we see light. [1]
For God, who said, "Let light shine out of darkness,"
made his light shine in our hearts to give us the light
of the knowledge of God's glory displayed in the face of Christ. [2]
For light shines on the righteous and joy on the upright in heart. [3]
In the same way, let our light shine before others,
that they may see our good deeds and glorify our Father in heaven. [4]

In Jesus Name,
Amen

The Protection of God

"As for us, the Lord is our God, and we have not forsaken him. The priests who serve the Lord are sons of Aaron, and the Levites assist them. Every morning and evening they present burnt offerings and fragrant incense to the Lord. They set out the bread on the ceremonially clean table and light the lamps on the gold lampstand every evening. We are observing the requirements of the Lord our God. But you have forsaken him. God is with us; he is our leader. His priests with their trumpets will sound the battle cry against you. People of Israel, do not fight against the Lord, the God of your ancestors, for you will not succeed."

2 Chronicles 13:10-12

We all face adversity and have enemies that attack us on the right and the left. The difference is that when we face adversity, we rely on the faithful protection and direction of God.

Your word is a lamp unto my feet and a light unto my path. I have taken an oath and confirmed it, that I will follow your righteous laws. I have suffered much; preserve my life, Lord, according to your word. Accept, Lord, the willing praise of my mouth, and teach me your laws. Though I constantly take my life in my hands, I will not forget your law. The wicked have set a snare for me, but I have not strayed from your precepts. Your statutes are my heritage forever; they are the joy of my heart. My heart is set on keeping your decrees to the very end.

Psalm 119:105 - 112

In HIS Light

During the reign of Solomon, two of the twelve tribes were separated from the others, making the tribes of Judah and the tribes of Israel. Abijah was king in Judah. Jeroboam was king in Israel. The tribes of Judah worshipped God, the tribes of Israel worshipped false gods. A war broke out between them.

Israel was armed with eight hundred thousand soldiers, Judah had four hundred thousand.

King Abijah of Judah spoke with great confidence, warning his enemy, Jeroboam, the battle would not end in his favor because the Israelites did not worship or trust God, but instead relied on golden calves and false gods.

As King Abijah spoke a warning to the tribes of Israel, the armies of Israel forged a strategic approach, an ambush, surrounding Judah in front and back. As the armies of Judah witnessed this, they cried out to God for help. At the sound of their battle cry, the Lord struck their enemy and more then five hundred thousand of their troops were slain.

> The Israelites were subdued on that occasion, and the people of Judah were victorious because they relied on the Lord, the God of their ancestors.
>
> 2 Chronicles 13:18

When we find ourselves surrounded by our enemy, we can rely on God to fight the battle.

In HIS Light

We choose to walk with Jesus that we may grow in His Light.

Most Gracious and Heavenly Father,

*We praise you and thank you for your endless love, mercy, and grace.
For with you is the fountain of life; in your light we see light.* [1]
*For God, who said, "Let light shine out of darkness,"
made his light shine in our hearts to give us the light
of the knowledge of God's glory displayed in the face of Christ.* [2]
For light shines on the righteous and joy on the upright in heart. [3]
*In the same way, let our light shine before others,
that they may see our good deeds and glorify our Father in heaven.* [4]

*In Jesus Name,
Amen*

God Will Never Disappoint

The Lord is my light and my salvation—whom shall I fear? The Lord is the stronghold of my life—of whom shall I be afraid?

Psalm 27:1

David penned Psalm 27 right before he was anointed to be king. As a young man, with brothers that served on the battlefield, I am certain David was no stranger to warfare. As a shepherd, David was tasked with the responsibility of caring for his flock.

This psalm reflects David's adoration, trust, and respect for God. David loved God with his whole heart, so much so that he just wanted to be in God's presence as much as possible. He trusted God with his life, and rather than fear his enemies, he simply asked God for protection and direction.

He also realized that we are erroneous people who commit sins regularly, therefore he asked for God's forgiveness and acknowledged God's desire to be seen, face-to-face. So often, we just want God to solve our problem and make the issues go away. We seek his hand instead of his face, but God desires for us to desire him.

In HIS Light

David also recognizes that there are enemies lying in wait, ready to attack. So he asks God to show him the Lord's way, to navigate him through the battlefields.

Finally, David shares that we are to be patiently connected to God in every way so that we refuse to give up and stand firmly in hope. Because God is faithful, he will never disappoint us.

We choose to walk with Jesus that we may grow in His Light.

Most Gracious and Heavenly Father,

We praise you and thank you for your endless love, mercy, and grace.
For with you is the fountain of life; in your light we see light. [1]
For God, who said, "Let light shine out of darkness,"
made his light shine in our hearts to give us the light
of the knowledge of God's glory displayed in the face of Christ. [2]
For light shines on the righteous and joy on the upright in heart. [3]
In the same way, let our light shine before others,
that they may see our good deeds and glorify our Father in heaven. [4]

In Jesus Name,
Amen

Armor of Light

The night is nearly over; the day is almost here. So let us put aside the deeds of darkness and put on the armor of light.

Romans 13:12

There will be a time when the Lord returns to the earth, and forms a new earth and a new heaven. When he arrives, like the maidens with lamps, we want to have enough oil to be ready when he appears.

Our obedience to authority is tantamount in being light. For those who do what they are told are bright lights that bring peace and security to those in authority. But those who do what they see fit as opposed to doing what they were instructed to do, become thorns in the side of those in authority.

God is the one who assigns authority to us. Those in authority over us are those who God has ordained. When we rebel against them, we rebel against God. Therefore, we are to submit to authority - whether it be a boss, parent, or governing body.

This is the will of God.

In HIS Light

We choose to walk with Jesus that we may grow in His Light.

Most Gracious and Heavenly Father,

We praise you and thank you for your endless love, mercy, and grace.
For with you is the fountain of life; in your light we see light. [1]
For God, who said, "Let light shine out of darkness,"
made his light shine in our hearts to give us the light
of the knowledge of God's glory displayed in the face of Christ. [2]
For light shines on the righteous and joy on the upright in heart. [3]
In the same way, let our light shine before others,
that they may see our good deeds and glorify our Father in heaven. [4]

In Jesus Name,
Amen

Share Your Light With Others

Light is sweet, and it pleases the eyes to see the sun. However many years anyone may live, let them enjoy them all. But let them remember the days of darkness, for there will be many. Everything to come is meaningless.
Ecclesiastes 11:7-8

Life is meant to be enjoyed. Our ability to enjoy life stems from many different aspects. We can enjoy people, our way of making a living, our generosity, and our way of relaxing. We especially enjoy life when we share our light with others.

Sharing our light translates into sharing our time, resources, and creative thought to resolve issues, celebrate successes, and show up for others in their time of need.

When we decide to share our light with others, it frees us to become more. We can give what we have and what we know that others may continue the work we have done and we can explore new avenues to venture into.

In the same way we share light, we can also share darkness. Our darkness translates to any evil, disrespectful, intentional maliciousness, or other acts intended to harm others. God will hold us to account for every action we take. It is

In HIS Light

up to us to choose wisely.

We choose to walk with Jesus that we may grow in His Light.

Most Gracious and Heavenly Father,

*We praise you and thank you for your endless love, mercy, and grace.
For with you is the fountain of life; in your light we see light.* [1]
*For God, who said, "Let light shine out of darkness,"
made his light shine in our hearts to give us the light
of the knowledge of God's glory displayed in the face of Christ.* [2]
For light shines on the righteous and joy on the upright in heart. [3]
*In the same way, let our light shine before others,
that they may see our good deeds and glorify our Father in heaven.* [4]

*In Jesus Name,
Amen*

Called Out of Darkness

But you are a chosen generation, a royal priesthood, a holy nation, a people set at liberty; so that you would show forth the virtues of the One Who has called you out of darkness into His marvelous light, in the past, you were not a people, yet are now the people of God; who in the past were not under mercy, but now have obtained mercy.

1 Peter 2:9-10

In Mark, chapter 13, the disciples were leaving the temple as one of the men admired it's construction, pointing out the beauty of the stones. Jesus told him that the temple would be completely destroyed in its future. Later as Jesus, Peter, James, Andrew and John were sitting on the Mount of Olives, across from the temple, the men asked Jesus when such things would occur. Jesus informed them that there would be signs of things to come, to signify the onslaught of the end times. Then he warned of the signs, and instructed every believer to ensure they were doing what they were called to do.

In 1 Peter, chapter 2, there is discussion of the chief cornerstone that the builders rejected which is a parable about Jesus, who was rejected by the Jews and accepted by the Gentiles. Jesus was a good man doing good things, yet he found himself asubject to the hatred of many men, especially those in authority, who wanted to see him dead.

Much like Jesus, we are asubject to unfair treatment. Even more like Jesus, we are to respond to such treatment with respect and endurance, allowng those in authority to have their way, regardless of its fairness. This is the will of God. Vengeance belongs to God, he will repay.

We have been called out of darkness and are saved by grace through faith in Jesus. We have received mercy, therefore, like Jesus we are to extend mercy to those who wrongfully persecute us. This can only be done when we seek God day and night, for we are being developed when we study the Word and as we commune with the Holy Spirit.

We choose to walk with Jesus that we may grow in His Light.

Most Gracious and Heavenly Father,

We praise you and thank you for your endless love, mercy, and grace.
For with you is the fountain of life; in your light we see light. [1]
For God, who said, "Let light shine out of darkness,"
made his light shine in our hearts to give us the light
of the knowledge of God's glory displayed in the face of Christ. [2]
For light shines on the righteous and joy on the upright in heart. [3]
In the same way, let our light shine before others,
that they may see our good deeds and glorify our Father in heaven. [4]

In Jesus Name,
Amen

Tried By Fire

If anyone builds on this foundation using gold, silver, costly stones, wood, hay or straw, their work will be shown for what it is, because the Day will bring it to light. It will be revealed with fire, and the fire will test the quality of each person's work.

1 Corinthians 3:12-13

As a part of the body of Christ, we each have our ordained responsibilities. As Paul writes, one plants, another waters, but it is God who makes it to grow. Therefore, there is no need for us to try and take credit for the blessing of growth in another. It is God himself who gets credit, for it is God who saved, encouraged, appointed and anointed each of us, and it is he who grants us life. As we build, all that we do should be laid upon a foundation in Christ which will stand in the face of adversity and beyond the scope of time.

It is also God who inspects the heart and is therefore able to correctly identify the motive behind our actions. We who are petty (arguing for vanity's sake) and still drinking milk (lacking the maturity to trust God regardless of recognition) are not equipped to judge a situation by its depth or width or height but can only judge based on its face value rendering us no judge at all. We are to leave all judgment to the Lord and the Lord alone.

In HIS Light

Ironically, many who are and have been blessed, sit in the seat of judgment. But as a warning, this is not right, for God's people are called to worship him through sacrifice, through the lending of all that we have that others may grow in him. As Paul, a fellow prisoner in Christ shared,

> For it seems to me that God has put us apostles on display at the end of the procession, like those condemned to die in the arena. We have been made a spectacle to the whole universe, to angels as well as to human beings. We are fools for Christ, but you are so wise in Christ! We are weak, but you are strong! You are honored, we are dishonored! To this very hour we go hungry and thirsty, we are in rags, we are brutally treated, we are homeless. We work hard with our own hands. When we are cursed, we bless; when we are persecuted, we endure it; when we are slandered, we answer kindly. We have become the scum of the earth, the garbage of the world—right up to this moment.
>
> I Corinthians 4:9-13

As true ambassadors of Christ, we are to walk in humility honoring those who work faithfully and tirelessly for the kingdom of God. It is arrogant and ignorant to do anything else, for we are tried by the fire. The Lord himself inspects the motive within our hearts and it is he who will sit in the seat of judgment on the day of reckoning, a day in which we will want to receive his love and a gentle spirit as opposed to the rod of discipline. We are all a part of the body of Christ and his temple is of great value, therefore we are not to destroy the body of Christ but to nourish and uplift.

> Do not deceive yourselves. If any of you think you are wise by the standards of this age, you should become "fools" so that you may become wise. For the wisdom of this world is foolishness in God's sight. As it is written: "He catches the wise in their craftiness"; and again, "The Lord knows that the thoughts of the wise are futile." So then, no more boasting about human leaders! All things are yours, whether Paul or Apollos or Cephas or the world or life or death or the present or the future—all are yours, and you are of Christ, and Christ is of God.
>
> I Corinthians 3:18-20

Instead of jealousy, judgment, trickery, disrespect, or

In HIS Light

the willful manipulation of those serving the body of Christ, we are to uplift, encourage, and celebrate those who sacrifice their all that others may live in the love of God and with the acknowledgement of Christ as our Savior.

We choose to walk with Jesus that we may grow in His Light.

Most Gracious and Heavenly Father,

We praise you and thank you for your endless love, mercy, and grace.
For with you is the fountain of life; in your light we see light. [1]
For God, who said, "Let light shine out of darkness,"
made his light shine in our hearts to give us the light
of the knowledge of God's glory displayed in the face of Christ. [2]
For light shines on the righteous and joy on the upright in heart. [3]
In the same way, let our light shine before others,
that they may see our good deeds and glorify our Father in heaven. [4]

In Jesus Name,
Amen

Joy, Wisdom & Enlightenment

The precepts of the Lord are right, giving joy to the heart. The commands of the Lord are radiant, giving light to the eyes.

Psalm 19:8

God has a way of making all things beautiful and purposeful. Even his laws are wonderful, they protect us from our poor decision-making in emotional states. Nature stands before us as an example of who God is - consistent, committed, and caring.

The sun rises and sets each day. The moon reveals itself according to the tide. Trees face seasonal growth and shedding. Nature is if nothing else, consistent and committed to the purpose God has laid out for it. Without nature, we would not be able to eat, create shelter, or survive.

There is, however, an element of chaos in nature, in that storms arise when we least expect them, but this is not of God. It is allowed by God but not of God, despite the contractual definition indemnifying responsibility and accountability during these weather burps called a "force majeure", known as an act of God. No, in fact, when storms arise it is evidence of

In HIS Light

a demonic force in the region. This is can be argued as when Jesus rebuked the wind (in Mark 4) and forced the skies to be still, while on his way to release a man burdened with demons who called themselves "legion." Those demons begged Jesus not to send them out of the region, and it seems the storm arose to keep Jesus from reaching their destination and completing his task.

    God has granted us access to the history and life of Jesus Christ, through the Old and New Testament. The Bible is full of not only what is right and what is wrong, but through stories exemplifies the application of both right and wrong decision-making. From the couple who refused to share their increase with the local church, to Jonah swept up in the whale, to Elijah calling down fire from heaven, we see how trusting God and doing what he commands is of great benefit to us.

    So what of the many laws, precepts, rules and structure God has given? As David writes in Psalm 19, when we appreciate and abide by them, they bring us joy, provide wisdom, enlighten us and keep us holy before God.

    God knows that we are not perfect beings. From Adam eating forbidden fruit, to Abraham and his wife taking matters into their own hands and birthing a son out of wedlock, to Moses killing an Egyptian slave master, to David killing an honorable man to take his wife, God knows we are not perfect beings. This is why he sent our Savior, Jesus Christ, to redeem us from a life of sin, to provide us with the gift of the Holy Spirit to help us when we fail.

    Many find fault in the law because they do not like to think of themselves as doing anything wrong, but the truth is that sin negatively impacts those we care about most, and the law often stands as a mirror, reflecting what we hate to acknowledge. If we

In HIS Light

can accept this truth, we can walk in the light. We do not have to be perfect to enjoy God, or his consistency, or his commitment to be faithful, all we must do is acknowledge him through our obedience, reverent worship, and praise because we know he lives.

Jesus loves us. It is his good pleasure to grant us the desires of our heart. But we must be willing to face the truth of who we are and how we show up. We must be willing to acknowledge our failures and course correct that God may be honored.

When times are hard and we face opposition, we can repeat the following statute David penned at the end of Psalm 19.

May these words of my mouth and this meditation of my heart be pleasing in your sight, Lord, my Rock and my Redeemer.
Psalm 19:14

We choose to walk with Jesus that we may grow in His Light.

Most Gracious and Heavenly Father,

We praise you and thank you for your endless love, mercy, and grace.
For with you is the fountain of life; in your light we see light. [1]
For God, who said, "Let light shine out of darkness,"
made his light shine in our hearts to give us the light
of the knowledge of God's glory displayed in the face of Christ. [2]
For light shines on the righteous and joy on the upright in heart. [3]
In the same way, let our light shine before others,
that they may see our good deeds and glorify our Father in heaven. [4]

In Jesus Name,
Amen

Acutely Aware

You are all children of the light and children of the day. We do not belong to the night or to the darkness. So then, let us not be like others, who are asleep, but let us be awake and sober.
I Thessalonians 5:5-6

We all have different personalities. Each of us march to the beat of our own drum. At times, our personalities clash like cymbals, not necessarily making music but certainly creating sound. We can avoid chaos if we learn to relate as individuals, acknowledge one anothers position, and encourage our fellow journeymen.

While chaos, disruption, and adversity are certain from time to time, we have the ability to course correct and shift our mindset to one that aligns with the will of God. Not only is this wise, it is life-saving advice.

We know that God is not going to post on social media the day he will return. He is not going to run ads in the local paper, or spots on the radio, encouraging people to live right. Instead, God will come like a thief in the night, and it will be a day of darkness. Therefore we are called to be a light, sober-minded and ready, seeking God, and always ready to hear a word from

In HIS Light

the Lord.

    As we wake to seek God's face, and desire his will above our own, we will approach life with a different level of optimism. Even in dark times, we will see his light as an encouragement to continue with faith. We will share joy with others, meet them where they are, and help them to get to their intended destination.

    It takes courage to walk in faith. It takes perseverance to smile each day in the face of adversity. It takes resilience to get up and try again after many days of failure and results that do not render what we desire. But God. God is here with us each day. God is able to open our eyes to see what hasn't been seen before. We can trust him even when life appears to fight us at every turn.

    We must remember the battle belongs to God and when we face storms, they are simply serving as obstacles to keep us from enjoying life, sharing the love of God, and experiencing God's best.

In HIS Light

We choose to walk with Jesus that we may grow in His Light.

Most Gracious and Heavenly Father,

We praise you and thank you for your endless love, mercy, and grace.
For with you is the fountain of life; in your light we see light. [1]
For God, who said, "Let light shine out of darkness,"
made his light shine in our hearts to give us the light
of the knowledge of God's glory displayed in the face of Christ. [2]
For light shines on the righteous and joy on the upright in heart. [3]
In the same way, let our light shine before others,
that they may see our good deeds and glorify our Father in heaven. [4]

In Jesus Name,
Amen

Stephanie D. Moore

Jesus at the Head

For he has rescued us from the dominion of darkness and brought us into the kingdom of the Son he loves, in whom we have redemption, the forgiveness of sins.

Colossians 1:13

Beginning our day with prayer, praise, and petitions before God is good and healthy. It reflects that we recognize our lives are in his hands. It identifies God as a sovereign authority in our lives. If we operate in this way with consistency, we will see our lives shift in a way that all around us will recognize God as our head.

It can be compared to a person who works out. If they work out on a regular basis, in some way it becomes recognizable to others without the person actually saying, "I work out every day." Instead, people begin to approach them saying, "What do you do to stay in such great shape?"

This is how the kingdom of God is to be reflected in our lives. People should recognize a uniqueness about us that makes them question, "How do you do it?"

In HIS Light

Our consistent behavior and spiritual workout opens the door to introduce Christ.

God has an amazing way of shining light and bringing clarity to a situation. We all suffer seasons of self-loathing, wondering if we are valuable, enough, or operating at our best. We tend to look back over every bad decision in our lives and paint a picture of ourselves that is disharmonious with the image God created us in. This is when we look outward, trying to find a beacon of light that can help us navigate back to a healthy place of self-reflection.

God, who loves us immensely, is always standing at the door, knocking, wishing to be let in. He wants to shine a light in the darkness that we may understand the state of our affairs, who we are and more importantly, who he has created us to be. When we worship God with consistency, living a life that honors God, we help others open the door to Christ.

This is how I was helped. I grew up in church, but lacked in faith because life was hard. One day, a good friend questioned my faith and encouraged me to believe. As I began to believe, I saw measurable change, I welcomed God and began to seek him. My life has never been the same. This is the blessing of Jesus, who is faithful, to guide and protect us. This is the blessing of the Holy Spirit, who prays for us when we do not know what to pray for. When we walk in the will of God, we not only help ourselves, we help others by sharing our faith.

A life of willful sin can lead to a life of needless suffering. A life of willful sin not only impacts the sinner but those closest to the sinner as well. Sin is pervasive and subtle. A lie here, a line of coke there, a one-night stand... all sins bear markable scars on our souls. But Christ died that we might live, and as we turn to Christ as our head, we not only help ourselves and those we love

In HIS Light

most, we help others to receive the gift of life as well.

We choose to walk with Jesus that we may grow in His Light.

Most Gracious and Heavenly Father,

We praise you and thank you for your endless love, mercy, and grace.
For with you is the fountain of life; in your light we see light. [1]
For God, who said, "Let light shine out of darkness,"
made his light shine in our hearts to give us the light
of the knowledge of God's glory displayed in the face of Christ. [2]
For light shines on the righteous and joy on the upright in heart. [3]
In the same way, let our light shine before others,
that they may see our good deeds and glorify our Father in heaven. [4]

In Jesus Name,
Amen

In Your Light

For with you is the fountain of life; in your light we see light.
Psalm 36:9

There was a commercial in which a woman, older in age, would fall, and say, "Help! I've fallen and I can't get up!"

This is the cry of a backslider found swirling down the drain of sin. One who has found themselves entangled in a series of poor choices that have led to a lifestyle of destruction. The question becomes, who do you call?

A life reverent to God hates sin. A person committed to God refuses to walk in darkness. Yet, so many Christians find themselves like that woman in the commercial. Crying out to God, "Lord, help me. I have fallen and I can't get up!"

It is difficult to be self-aware and recognize when we are beginning to make decisions that impede our walk with God. Our light dims before it completely diminishes and gets dark. We can be hypercritical and hypocrites without recognizing that we too are lost in our own downward spirals of sin with no room to judge or point a finger at anyone else. We can think so highly

In HIS Light

of ourselves that we tend to ignore our sin or minimize the fact that our actions are in fact, sin.

Thank God that we are not judged by our sins. When we have accepted Christ as our savior, we have the ability to confess our sins and pray for forgiveness. Rather than be graded, we receive grace. It is his love that keeps us, and his love that protects us. It is his faithful heart and generous nature that extend to us, unending mercy and grace.

For it is only in his light that we can see light.

We choose to walk with Jesus that we may grow in His Light.

Most Gracious and Heavenly Father,

We praise you and thank you for your endless love, mercy, and grace. For with you is the fountain of life; in your light we see light. [1]
For God, who said, "Let light shine out of darkness," made his light shine in our hearts to give us the light of the knowledge of God's glory displayed in the face of Christ. [2]
For light shines on the righteous and joy on the upright in heart. [3]
In the same way, let our light shine before others, that they may see our good deeds and glorify our Father in heaven. [4]

In Jesus Name,
Amen

A New Walk

We also have the prophetic message as something completely reliable, and you will do well to pay attention to it, as to a light shining in a dark place, until the day dawns and the morning star rises in your hearts. Above all, you must understand that no prophecy of Scripture came about by the prophet's own interpretation of things. For prophecy never had its origin in the human will, but prophets, though human, spoke from God as they were carried along by the Holy Spirit.

2 Peter 1:19-21

When I was a little girl, I often heard the members of our church sing, "Please, be patient with me, God is not through with me yet!"

As we walk with Jesus, we learn and desire to become more and more like him each day. This means there are attributes we adopt and uphold as sacred and holy. Not only are we doing it because we know it is right, but we do it because we want to please God, who is faithful in his promises toward us.

With God, there is a seed of faith, sometimes it is just a mustard seed, but that is all we need to believe. If we believe nothing is impossible with God, we can see all things according to his will come to pass.

In HIS Light

"For all the promises of God in Him are Yes, and in Him Amen,
to the glory of God through us."

2 Corinthians 1:20

God is also good, therefore, as we walk with God we are good to ourselves and good to others. But that requires that we understand the difference between good and evil, which is impossible without knowledge. Knowledge of God's word, knowledge of those we are connected to, those we serve, and have been ordained to bless with the presence of God.

Self-control or the ability to say no when it is necessary (to negative activity or influence) and yes when it is required (such as paying taxes, exercising, or telling the truth even when it is difficult). Self-control was reflected when Jesus refused the temptation of Satan in the wilderness, when he said yes to turning the water into wine at the wedding at his mother's request, and when he returned the soldiers ear after Peter cut it off.

Perseverance in the face of adversity is yet another attribute we develop as we walk with God. Without a doubt, every person walking this earth will face adversity. How we handle adversity is the key. Sometimes, simply showing up is an answer to adversity and reflects our confidence in God to see us through. We persevere in strength with God at our side, and his angels encamped around us in protection. Jesus goes before us and makes every crooked place straight, and because our battles belong to God, all we have to do is persevere. The power of the Holy Spirit resides in us, so when we are scrutinized and questioned, we can rely on God who has the answer.

Godliness is an attribute that comes after a season of God showing that he is faithful. I don't believe anyone simply

In HIS Light

turns about face, until there is an encounter with God that is life-changing. But in that road to Damascus experience, God powerfully makes himself and his power known to us and we choose a life of godliness in reverence to the omnipotent, omniscient, and omnibenovolent presence of God. We may stumble, but we do not fall.

We also develop a mutual affection of respect and friendliness toward others. God is no respecter of persons, meaning he sees us all the same. As people of God, we see everyone as a person walking in life. We do not dismiss the homeless or those who do not believe in the same way that we do. Every person alive has the breath of God in them, meaning there is still hope for God's love to shine brightly in their hearts. It is up to us to treat them with the same honor, love, and respect that God would should them, therefore an encounter with us is to be as an encounter with God (for we are his hands and feet in the earth).

Finally, we are to love ourselves and others. Love manifests itself in many ways. But it is the gift of generosity that opens the heart of revelation for many that they are indeed loved.

> For God so loved the world, that he gave his only begotten son, that whosoever believed in him, would have everlasting life.
> John 3:16

Generosity is most appreciated when we do not deserve it. When people continue to give to us despite our sense of entitlement or lack of reciprocity, we thank God for their generosity. For it is by the gift of generosity when we least deserve it that we see "forgiveness" for what it actually is. It is an undeserved gift, it is the definition of mercy, and the experience of grace. It is a reflection of the light of God as we walk with him and allow him to guide our decision-making process. It is why

In HIS Light

we show up again and again, each day, praying God will see us through. Generosity is a ray of sunshine piercing through a dark night.

As we walk with God, we worship God in wholeness and truth. We seek him while he may be found. We acknowledge his Word as truth. We allow his Holy Spirit to embody us with his will and to provide us with clear direction.

We choose to walk with Jesus that we may grow in His Light.

Most Gracious and Heavenly Father,

*We praise you and thank you for your endless love, mercy, and grace.
For with you is the fountain of life; in your light we see light.* [1]
*For God, who said, "Let light shine out of darkness,"
made his light shine in our hearts to give us the light
of the knowledge of God's glory displayed in the face of Christ.* [2]
For light shines on the righteous and joy on the upright in heart. [3]
*In the same way, let our light shine before others,
that they may see our good deeds and glorify our Father in heaven.* [4]

*In Jesus Name,
Amen*

Light is Love

Your eye is the lamp of your body. When your eyes are healthy, your whole body also is full of light. But when they are unhealthy, your body also is full of darkness.

Luke 11:34

The love of God shines a bright light into our lives that we want to share with others. For we have received the love of God like a child. When we have a need, we pray to God for guidance, provision, protection and direction. We honor God as we pray, just as we would honor a parent when we ask for help. We reverence God first and acknowledge that he is sovereign. We pray that his needs and desires are met before ours, his will to be done in the earth just as it is in heaven. Then we ask God to grant us an abundance of the bread of life, his Word. We ask for the will to forgive as we have been forgiven and the ability and discipline to turn away from sin. As we finish our prayer, we again remind God that he is the only one we reverence as ruler of all. God who is faithful, will grant us what we ask for because we asked him.

Love heals. But everyone does not appreciate the power to heal or the gift of empowerment. Dark eyes take good things and return them with mediocrity. Dark eyes misuse and abuse those who trust them. But God's light is love, it empowers and

In HIS Light

uplifts. Lights shine brightly before others giving guidance and direction.

But darkness calls love failure, generosity a burden, and greed empowerment. For this reason, those who help the homeless, or dedicate their lives to serving the vulnerable are looked at as less than intelligent, dishonorable, and disengaged from reality. However, Jesus taught us that it is not the outside of a man that makes them unclean, but the inside that flows outward in hatred, total disregard, disrespect, and dishonor that makes a man unclean.

God has called each of us out of darkness into his marvellous light. But it is up to us to choose to walk in the light, dismissing discussions that require the poor to celebrate us when we give mediocre gifts, or that we be lifted up that all men may bow in our presence because we have achieved a level of success that required the blood, sweat and tears of others that we may gain. Instead, God has called us to give rather than receive, to love rather than hate, and to honor and respect those whom society deems dishonorable and disrespectful.

As God gives his light to us, we too must be willing to give our light to others.

In HIS Light

We choose to walk with Jesus that we may grow in His Light.

Most Gracious and Heavenly Father,

We praise you and thank you for your endless love, mercy, and grace.
For with you is the fountain of life; in your light we see light. [1]
For God, who said, "Let light shine out of darkness,"
made his light shine in our hearts to give us the light
of the knowledge of God's glory displayed in the face of Christ. [2]
For light shines on the righteous and joy on the upright in heart. [3]
In the same way, let our light shine before others,
that they may see our good deeds and glorify our Father in heaven. [4]

In Jesus Name,
Amen

Speak Light

Light in a messenger's eyes brings joy to the heart, and good news gives health to the bones.

Proverbs 15:30

Words are containers of power that echo over time. The lifespan of a communication can impact the hearers, speakers, and those they influence for generations. We must choose our words wisely.

Therefore as communicators, it is more important to check our hearts, and ensure we have the right heart space before we share what is on our mind.

"Make a tree good and its fruit will be good, or make a tree bad and its fruit will be bad, for a tree is recognized by its fruit. You brood of vipers, how can you who are evil say anything good? For the mouth speaks what the heart is full of. A good man brings good things out of the good stored up in him, and an evil man brings evil things out of the evil stored up in him. But I tell you that everyone will have to give account on the day of judgment for every empty word they have spoken. For by your words you will be acquitted, and by your words you will be condemned."

Matthew 12:33-37

Proverbs 15 shares some key insights regarding

In HIS Light

communications, we can use as a quick guide.

- God is paying attention to what we say. God spoke all that we see and know into existence by the power of his word. Jesus is the Word of God. God created us in his likeness, therefore, when we speak, we create.

- Harsh words crush those who hear them, we must learn to communicate the truth with grace. We can either create conflict or encourage peace, we choose by what we say and how we say it.

- Greed destroys families.

- The wise continue on the path as directed, but those who love disruption, destruction, and disgrace are unwise.

- Humility comes before honor, it is wise to fear the Lord. - Proverbs 15:33

- "Mockers resent correction, they avoid the wise." - Proverbs 15:12

- "The discerning heart seeks knowledge, but the mouth of a fool feeds on folly." - Proverbs 15:14

- "The Lord tears down the house of the proud, but he sets the widow's boundary stones in place." Proverbs 15:26

- "A wise son brings joy to his father, but a foolish man despises his mother." - Proverbs 15:20

When we speak, we are to let our words be seasoned with salt, giving flavor to a conversation that is edifying and good for ns who hear it.

In HIS Light

We choose to walk with Jesus that we may grow in His Light.

Most Gracious and Heavenly Father,

We praise you and thank you for your endless love, mercy, and grace.
For with you is the fountain of life; in your light we see light. [1]
For God, who said, "Let light shine out of darkness,"
made his light shine in our hearts to give us the light
of the knowledge of God's glory displayed in the face of Christ. [2]
For light shines on the righteous and joy on the upright in heart. [3]
In the same way, let our light shine before others,
that they may see our good deeds and glorify our Father in heaven. [4]

In Jesus Name,
Amen

The Light of God

Command the Israelites to bring you clear oil of pressed olives for the light so that the lamps may be kept burning continually.
Leviticus 24:2

Leviticus 24 is broken down to reflect three key concepts in the Old Testament that are directly connected to our daily worship and the sacrifice of Jesus Christ. We are to worship God in wholeness and truth, regardless of what is required of us. This may mean that we tend to the fire of our lamps all night, bring a consistent tithe to ensure those who minister among us are able to provide guidance, and finally, the physical sacrifice of submission to the will of God, being the commitment of our lives in worship (our reasonable service).

1.   Lamps & Light

The lamps within and without the tabernacle were to be kept lit. This required a commitment of time and attention, and for the people to provide the oil. It is symbolic of the Holy Spirit in our lives which helps us to see where we are, where we are going, and why it is important for us to submit to the will of God. The Holy Spirit even prays for us in ways we do not understand but is for our good.

# In HIS Light

2. Bread of Life

The bread was to be stacked in 12 loaves each week on the Sabbath day. It represents the Word of God, which is to be eaten by the priests each week and stands as the holiest of meals for them. This bread of life, the Word of God, educates, empowers, and encompasses their belief system in a way that allows the priests to share the will of God with others as it is revealed to them in the Word of God. Jesus told his disciples to eat the bread which represented his body.

3. Sacrifice

When a local man, born of mixed heritage, fought with a local Israelite he blasphemed the name of God. The Israelite priests were unsure of how to approach the scenario, because of his heritage. The local priests consulted God for direction. God through Moses told them to stone the young man. In addition to instructing them to stone the young man for blasphemy, he also instructed them on how to handle the act of injury on another through the principle of "an eye for an eye."

Similarly, Jesus who was born to Mary, but whose father was recognized as Joseph, under the kingship lineage of David, but also whose birth father was unknown (due to Mary's sudden pregnancy when engaged to Joseph), came to earth as the child of God, but was accused of blasphemy by the local priests because he declared that he was the Son of Man. The Israelite priests were unsure of how to handle Jesus. The priests recalled the instruction of God, who told them to stone the one who took God's name in vain. The crucifixion of Jesus also exercised the principle of "an eye for an eye". Jesus had to die, as a sacrifice for our sins, a debt paid for us, that we might experience an eternal life without the consequence of sin and the benefit of walking with God.

The light of God shines within us, through the power

In HIS Light

of the Holy Spirit, refreshed by his Word daily, and solidified by the sacrifice of Jesus Christ. However, just as the people in Leviticus 24 had to supply the oil for the lamps, the flour for the loaves of bread, and were forced to stone the man, we too must participate in the process of worship in order to receive the benefits that Christ died for us to have. We must welcome the Holy Spirit, we must be intentional about feeding on the Word of God - the holiest of meals, and we must be willing to sacrifice our lives as Christ did for us that others may know God and receive his light.

We choose to walk with Jesus that we may grow in His Light.

Most Gracious and Heavenly Father,

We praise you and thank you for your endless love, mercy, and grace.
For with you is the fountain of life; in your light we see light. [1]
For God, who said, "Let light shine out of darkness,"
made his light shine in our hearts to give us the light
of the knowledge of God's glory displayed in the face of Christ. [2]
For light shines on the righteous and joy on the upright in heart. [3]
In the same way, let our light shine before others,
that they may see our good deeds and glorify our Father in heaven. [4]

In Jesus Name,
Amen

Freedom

"I, the Lord, have called you in righteousness; I will take hold of your hand. I will keep you and will make you to be a covenant for the people and a light for the Gentiles, to open eyes that are blind, to free captives from prison and to release from the dungeon those who sit in darkness."

Isaiah 42:6-7

The knowledge of God, acceptance of Jesus as our Savior, and receipt of the Holy Spirit grant us freedom from an inevitable life of sin that has been naturally passed down to us by our blood-born relatives. But this freedom can only be realized through relationship. Relationships operate in reciprocity. God treats us well. It is up to us to respond in kind.

Despite God's gracious gift of a life free from sin, we knowingly choose sin as our destination, over and over again. Rather than praise God and share in his love and light, we find ourselves seeking that which has no hope, which only offers fateful ends, convincing ourselves that we know life better than the God who created life... and we suffer from the fate of our own decisions.

But God.

In HIS Light

God sent Jesus because he recognized that we were spiritual beings trapped in earthly bodies that naturally seek out sin, despite knowing what is best and good for us. We make decisions that cause us harm rather than those which present good and honor God. It is true, we all love God in our minds and with our mouths, but it is the worship with our bodies that bear the greatest impact on our destinations.

It is our walk that matters most, therefore, it was the walk of Jesus that mattered most for us. As a perfect sacrifice for our sins, we have been given the freedom to fail. Jesus was a slave to our sin, not his own, living a life that exemplified God's presence, God's love, God's all powerful ability, and God's sovereignty that we might have hope.

Jesus is our light in a life filled with darkness. His Holy Spirit is a flame that burns within us, shining God's light within us to remind us that he loves us and that we are not without hope. Jesus left us the Holy Spirit as our helpmate because God knows that it is not good that man should walk alone.

Sin brings pain. We can deny it for as long as we like, but the truth is. Sin shatters not only our lives but also the lives of those who love us. Jesus came that we might have freedom from the burden of sin (not the consequence of sin), the guilt that comes from being a sinner, the unforgiving nature of judgment that we wallow in, not from others but that which resonates within ourselves. Without Jesus we would equate sin with failure but they are not the same, sin was strapped to our DNA at birth, it was Satan's path to accuse the brethren. But Jesus died that we may be forgiven, once and forever from sin, that we may live a life without guilt but one instead that is filled with hope, faith, and freedom.

In HIS Light

We choose to walk with Jesus that we may grow in His Light.

Most Gracious and Heavenly Father,

*We praise you and thank you for your endless love, mercy, and grace.
For with you is the fountain of life; in your light we see light.* [1]
*For God, who said, "Let light shine out of darkness,"
made his light shine in our hearts to give us the light
of the knowledge of God's glory displayed in the face of Christ.* [2]
For light shines on the righteous and joy on the upright in heart. [3]
*In the same way, let our light shine before others,
that they may see our good deeds and glorify our Father in heaven.* [4]

*In Jesus Name,
Amen*

The God of More than Enough

There are many who say, "Who will show us any good?"

Lord, lift up the light of Your countenance upon us. You have put gladness in my heart, More than in the season that their grain and wine increased. I will both lie down in peace, and sleep; For You alone, O Lord, make me dwell in safety.

Psalm 4:6-8

    We have been blessed to see another day. The breath of God still courses through our bodies, with the Spirit of God at the helm, guiding us. Yet, as insatiable creatures walking this earth, no matter how blessed we become, there is always a hunger for more.

    This comes in part from just being human, but it also comes from a spirit of comparison. Comparison leads to jealousy, jealousy leads to hatred, and hatred leads to poor behavior. For a believer, this is unbecoming, but also woefully unnecessary. As a believer, we are blessed beyond measure. We have spiritual gifts that cannot be compared to purses, jewelry, cars, or homes. We have the ability to save lives, to heal the sick and to save the lost. Everything else is a distraction from God.

In HIS Light

When we are favored by God, we know that we have been set apart. The sacrifice of righteousness is good enough for us, despite the wealth increase of those who willfully sin day and night, because we trust in God. We know that when we call on God, he hears us. We know that we don't have to fight our battles, we can just be still and allow God to do it.

We can trust God to grant the desires of our heart. It is not necessary to trick, scheme, manipulate or steal. We can walk in peace, with rest, knowing that God is always for us.

We choose to walk with Jesus that we may grow in His Light.

Most Gracious and Heavenly Father,

We praise you and thank you for your endless love, mercy, and grace.
For with you is the fountain of life; in your light we see light. [1]
For God, who said, "Let light shine out of darkness,"
made his light shine in our hearts to give us the light
of the knowledge of God's glory displayed in the face of Christ. [2]
For light shines on the righteous and joy on the upright in heart. [3]
In the same way, let our light shine before others,
that they may see our good deeds and glorify our Father in heaven. [4]

In Jesus Name,
Amen

From Darkness to Light

> Then Saul, still breathing threats and murder against the disciples of the Lord, went to the high priest and asked letters from him to the synagogues of Damascus, so that if he found any who were of the Way, whether men or women, he might bring them bound to Jerusalem. As he journeyed he came near Damascus, and suddenly a light shone around him from heaven. Then he fell to the ground, and heard a voice saying to him, "Saul, Saul, why are you persecuting Me?"
>
> Acts 9:1-4

We all suffer through moments or periods of pitch black. Sometimes, we stumble in the dark because darkness is all that we know - all that we were taught, or all that we were exposed to. Darkness can be a condition, a circumstance, or a consequence. Regardless of how darkness was allowed into our lives, the only solution is Christ.

God has a unique way of turning darkness into light. The countenance of God converts, heals, and restores life, leading many to believe. It is nothing short of glorious to all who bear witness.

Saul of Tarsus, a man well-known for his determination to destroy all those who believed in Jesus Christ, a witness and supporter of the murder of Stephen (a devout Christian and faithful leader), bore witness to the glory of God and was forever

In HIS Light

changed. At one time a zealous enemy of God (unknowingly so), Saul was filled with a darkness that he could not understand or admit. It was not until he was confronted by the Spirit of God on a road to Damascus, were his eyes opened to see his true position in the kingdom. What once was dark, became light. Paul was converted to a follower of Christ and became a powerful messenger for God. Many believed the word when Paul preached and gave their lives to Christ.

Peter saved a man, crippled, unable to walk and bedridden for eight years, in a moment. Witnesses believed and gave their lives to Christ. Peter also saved a woman, well-favored by her community, from the hands of death, quickly restoring her life. Many heard of the miracle, believed, and gave their lives to Christ. By the fear of God and the comfort of the Holy Spirit, the church prospered, obtained peace and grew exponentially.

Whether we meet God on a road to Damascus or encounter God as he heals the sick, raises the dead or simply allows peace and comfort to reign where chaos once ruled, an encounter with God can immediately convert our darkness into light. When we experience this life-giving light, not only are we saved, but those who are a witness believe as well.

In HIS Light

We choose to walk with Jesus that we may grow in His Light.

Most Gracious and Heavenly Father,

*We praise you and thank you for your endless love, mercy, and grace.
For with you is the fountain of life; in your light we see light.* [1]
*For God, who said, "Let light shine out of darkness,"
made his light shine in our hearts to give us the light
of the knowledge of God's glory displayed in the face of Christ.* [2]
For light shines on the righteous and joy on the upright in heart. [3]
*In the same way, let our light shine before others,
that they may see our good deeds and glorify our Father in heaven.* [4]

*In Jesus Name,
Amen*

Our God is a Consuming Fire

And have you completely forgotten this word of encouragement that addresses you as a father addresses his son? It says, "My son, do not make light of the Lord's discipline, and do not lose heart when he rebukes you, because the Lord disciplines the one he loves, and he chastens everyone he accepts as his son."

Hebrews 12:5-6

    For a very long time, the thought of living a holy life frightened me. It seemed and some days still seems like an impossible feat suited only for the son of God, our Savior, Jesus Christ. But to live holy, is to accept the righteousness of Jesus and to walk with Him day and night, doing our best to obey his will. It is not perfection, it is simply the serious and intentional pursuit of such that God has called us to.

    If we are not careful, bitterness will replace the efforts we make to become holy. There is no question that seeing the unrighteous gain can wear down every layer of protection and create a hole in our heart so large that it will seem as if everyone can see it and see through it.

    Endurance creates healing in places we did not know we were weak. If we can endure, we will cross the bridge that separates us from the peace of God that walking with him

In HIS Light

brings. But if we fail to listen to our heavenly Father as he guides us while we are still on earth, how can we possibly be trusted to listen to him in heaven? We have a decision to make.

Consider Esau, who, tired from a hard day of work gave up his birthright for a hot meal. When it was done, and it was time to receive his birthright, it was given away, and no matter how angry, upset, or repentant he was, he was not going to get his blessing back. This is an example of the kingdom of God. Once we give up our desire to be with God, and intentionally take actions that continuously separate us from God, we cannot get that blessing back - no matter how hard we try.

Sin is enjoyable in the moment and holiness at times, can feel like a burden, a cross to bear. But sin actually hurts us and those we love most, while holiness and the pursuit of such heals our souls and leads us into a place that invites God to commune with us. When we spend time with God, we experience a joy that cannot be described because he knows us, intimately, and can meet us where we are. When our ways please God, he will even make our enemies to be at peace with us.

God is not a volcano of emotion, ready to erupt at the sight of our presence. Instead, God is our resting place, our Sabbath, our peace, Mount Zion, where we can receive righteousness by the blood of Jesus. It is our responsibility, by the grace, mercy and favor of God, to hear the voice of Jesus when he calls. It is an honor to open the door when he knocks at our hearts. It is our privilege to receive instruction from the creator of all things. It is a gift to receive the love of our Savior, his light, and his forgiveness. We must learn to embrace, appreciate, and adhere to the careful direction of Jesus, less we choose by our own ignorance and indignation to face God, an all-consuming fire.

In HIS Light

We choose to walk with Jesus that we may grow in His Light.

Most Gracious and Heavenly Father,

We praise you and thank you for your endless love, mercy, and grace.
For with you is the fountain of life; in your light we see light. [1]
For God, who said, "Let light shine out of darkness,"
made his light shine in our hearts to give us the light
of the knowledge of God's glory displayed in the face of Christ. [2]
For light shines on the righteous and joy on the upright in heart. [3]
In the same way, let our light shine before others,
that they may see our good deeds and glorify our Father in heaven. [4]

In Jesus Name,
Amen

A Witness to the Light

In him was life, and that life was the light of all mankind.
The light shines in the darkness, and the darkness has not overcome it.

John 1:4-5

Jesus is the one, true, living son of God. There is no one else that can stake claim, nor any other by which we can receive salvation. Jesus is the way.

In the beginning was the Word, and the Word was with God, and the Word was God. He was with God in the beginning. Through him all things were made; without him nothing was made that has been made.

John 1:1-3

The world and all that we know was created by spoken word. God said, "Let there be light," and there was light. Jesus is the Word, therefore all that we know, imagine, and say are engrossed in the benevolent system of God, who created all things. We were created in the likeness of God. This is why the scripture says, "the power of life and death are in the tongue." We have the power to create and destroy with our words. It is a power given to us through the being and authority of Jesus Christ. This power is ours but we are not Christ and do not have his power.

In HIS Light

Our creator, in infinite wisdom, developed a system that could not be destroyed. No amount of science or sorcery are able to overcome the Word that is Jesus. Jesus is the light that shines in the darkness, creating awareness and a way of escape. Victory belongs to God. When we become aware of evil and it's actual ability to destroy our lives and the lives of those we love most, we desire to become better, more responsible, and hold ourselves accountable to what we know.

The Word studied and spoken has the power to protect, save, and give life. When we share the Word of God with others, we become a witness to the light. John the Baptist was a cousin to Jesus, but before Christ was known to the world, or baptized, John preached the gospel of repentance to many. When asked what his role in the kingdom was, he shared that he was the voice of one crying in the wilderness, creating a straight path for the Lord to travel.

As believers and carriers of the light of Christ, we too share in the responsibility of creating a straight path for the Lord to travel. Jesus is knocking at the door of every person's heart. He is ready and available to them, but he desires an introduction.

Introductions help to formulate trust. Consider friends or even business acquaintances you have met through the power of an introduction by someone you trust. When we testify about the goodness of Jesus to others, they let down their defense and become available to the love of Christ. Life and death are in what we say, therefore as witnesses of the light, we create life-giving introductions by the power of our testimony.

In HIS Light

We choose to walk with Jesus that we may grow in His Light.

Most Gracious and Heavenly Father,

*We praise you and thank you for your endless love, mercy, and grace.
For with you is the fountain of life; in your light we see light.* [1]
*For God, who said, "Let light shine out of darkness,"
made his light shine in our hearts to give us the light
of the knowledge of God's glory displayed in the face of Christ.* [2]
For light shines on the righteous and joy on the upright in heart. [3]
*In the same way, let our light shine before others,
that they may see our good deeds and glorify our Father in heaven.* [4]

*In Jesus Name,
Amen*

The Nature of Darkness

> By this time it was about noon, and darkness fell across the whole land until three o'clock. The light from the sun was gone. And suddenly, the curtain in the sanctuary of the Temple was torn down the middle. Then Jesus shouted, "Father, I entrust my spirit into your hands!" And with those words he breathed his last.
>
> Luke 23:44-46

There is an eerie feeling of uneasiness that comes over us when we stand in the dark. When it is pitch dark, without light, we can become afraid because we don't know what is there. When we are in the dark, it is our natural sensation to seek light.

Just as we get uneasy in visible dark, there is a darkness that can come over our lives, a sense that we are moving into the unknown. Whether it is COVID-19 silently spreading, mass shooters that seem to pop up everywhere we frequent in order to live (such as malls, churches, grocery stores, workplaces, and schools), financial burdens that gain in interest every moment we breathe, weight gain, hair loss, health crisis, or relationship strains… we can find ourselves sitting in the dark wondering, how do we get to the light?

We can even find ourselves sitting in the dark AS we walk with Jesus. This is a reality that many of us hate to face. We can live a life that is committed to placing God first in our

In HIS Light

time, finances, and considerations yet still feel like we are on a battlefield in the dark, trying to get to the light.

When Jesus was at his best, he suffered the most. Jesus had successfully trained twelve disciples in the work of the ministry, had many apostles sharing the word, healed the sick, raised the dead, and eloquently disected, served, and disseminated the message of the Bible while walking it out for many to see. Yet, he faced the rejection of his brothers, the threat of violence, the betrayal of those closest to him, and the reality that he would one day soon have to face the darkness alone. Jesus was ridiculed, beaten, and eventually murdered before a people he only wanted to help. Moments before he died, as all manner of lasciviousness surrounded him, he cried out to God.

> Jesus said, "Father, forgive them, for they don't know what they are doing." And the soldiers gambled for his clothes by throwing dice.
> Luke 23:34

This is a moment to stop and consider... did God leave us here to suffer needlessly and alone, wondering about, trying to create a life from what is left? How do we get back to joy, love, rest, and enjoyment? What is God trying to teach us in the moments when we are in the dark?

The last thing Jesus saw were men gambling for the remnants of his life.

Life is what we make it. While we may suffer needlessly because someone injured us, we are responsible for our healing and our response to the situation. Seasons of darkness can be pierced by rays of sunshine if we allow it, we are not relegated to simply fumbling about in the dark, God has more for us and he desires that we take advantage of it. Jesus died that we may obtain freedom from a life of sacrifice, disrespect, unhappiness,

In HIS Light

and pain.

> The crowd watched and the leaders scoffed. "He saved others," they said, "let him save himself if he is really God's Messiah, the Chosen One."
>
> Luke 23:35

    With God all things are possible to those who believe. People will not do what is right because they should. In an ideal world, people will recognize the pain they inflict and course correct. Unfortunately, the ugly truth is many people are selfish, greedy, and do not care whether we live or die. We can beg, plead, show them the truth, and they will turn their heads the other way. Jesus watched as people he helped yelled "Crucify him!" and freed a murderer, one who took life in exchange for the one who gave life.

    At the moment of Jesus' death, a darkness fell over the land.

> When the Roman officer overseeing the execution saw what had happened, he worshiped God and said, "Surely this man was innocent." And when all the crowd that came to see the crucifixion saw what had happened, they went home in deep sorrow. But Jesus' friends, including the women who had followed him from Galilee, stood at a distance watching.
>
> Luke 23:47-79

    We must be careful in how we treat ourselves and others. There is a layer of resentment and regret that cannot be washed away with time. It follows us. There are so many people walking with an indescribable pain, a hollow ringing in their souls that echoes as they rehearse the pain they caused or suffered over and over again.

In HIS Light

And the great dragon was cast out, that old serpent, called the Devil, and Satan, which deceiveth the whole world: he was cast out into the earth, and his angels were cast out with him.

And I heard a loud voice saying in heaven, Now is come salvation, and strength, and the kingdom of our God, and the power of his Christ: for the accuser of our brethren is cast down, which accused them before our God day and night.

And they overcame him by the blood of the Lamb, and by the word of their testimony; and they loved not their lives unto the death.

Revelation 12:9-11

The work of the enemy is to kill, steal, and destroy. When we intentionally walk with Jesus, we are not taking actions that unravel the fabric of the lives of others (be it family, friend, or stranger). If our actions lead to the harm of others, we are not walking with God, we are contributing to the work of the enemy. We cannot hope that God does what we know we are responsible to do. We will be held accountable for our actions, in life or in death... the choice is ours.

___We choose to walk with Jesus that we may grow in His Light.___

Most Gracious and Heavenly Father,

We praise you and thank you for your endless love, mercy, and grace.
For with you is the fountain of life; in your light we see light. [1]
For God, who said, "Let light shine out of darkness,"
made his light shine in our hearts to give us the light
of the knowledge of God's glory displayed in the face of Christ. [2]
For light shines on the righteous and joy on the upright in heart. [3]
In the same way, let our light shine before others,
that they may see our good deeds and glorify our Father in heaven. [4]

In Jesus Name,
Amen

Citations

1. Psalm 36:9
2. 2 Corinthians 4:6
3. Psalm 97:11
4. Matthew 5:16
5. https://ajr.edu/2018/05/behahalotekha/#:~:text=A%20priest%20must%20wave%20the,being%20waved%20belongs%20to%20God.

About the Author

At the age of 9, Stephanie was molested by a friend of my family. In high school, she held the hand of a friend as he died from a fatal gun shot wound… As an adult, she was the victim of a violent acquaintance rape. Subsequently, she struggled with personal demons. But when she sought the Lord and his Word, her life was forever changed.

Give God ALL the Glory!

He is and will always be the head of my life. He is my joy, my strength, my everything.
My constant prayer is to be a perfect conduit of his message and love.

Stephanie was born in Muskogee, Oklahoma. She graduated from Putnam City North High School in 1994. She was married for 16 years. She is the mother of 3 beautiful daughters, and has a grandson named Levi. She graduated with her Associates in Technology, a Bachelor of Arts in Communications, and a Master of Arts in Communication with an emphasis in Political Communication.

She holds several design and technology certifications and has won numerous awards in that area. Stephanie has worked in television, print and web media for more than 16 years.

She is the owner of Moore Marketing and Communications. Her company offers strategic marketing and communication plans, media purchases, public relations, writing services, print services, graphic design and web design. Stephanie has also served as a poltical consultant for Governor, Lt. Governor, State Representative, Mayoral and City Council candidates.

Stephanie has created and sponsored teen etiquette and leadership programs for young ladies and young men. The program for young ladies is called, She's a BOSSE (A Beautiful Oasis of Success, Style and Elegance) and the young man's program is called Grindaholix: Young Men on the Rise.

To date, Stephanie has authored 25 books, 16 of which are daily devotionals. To learn more, visit mooretoread.com.

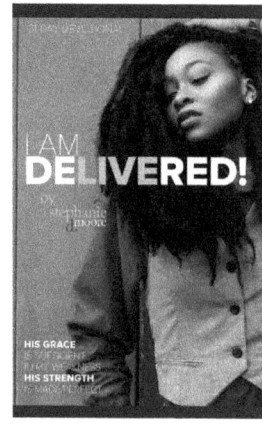

www.ingramcontent.com/pod-product-compliance
Lightning Source LLC
Chambersburg PA
CBHW060813050426
42449CB00008B/1652